Hopes and Fears
Learning Academically in a COVID-19 Environment

Published by Glenda D. Moton, M.Ed.
Text Copyright: © Glenda D. Moton, M.Ed.

ISBN – 978-0-578-97004-5

Table of Contents

Dedication

This project is dedicated to the students, staff, and administrators at North Miami Senior High School. Although this school year has been one of many challenges, your determination and efforts are to be commended during this global pandemic.

"May your choices reflect your Hopes, not your Fears." – Nelson Mandela

Meet the Editors

Glenda Moton

Ms. Glenda Moton is originally from Cincinnati, Ohio, but was raised in Miami, Florida, where she attended and graduated from Miami Northwestern Sr. High school. After graduating from high school, she attended Tennessee State University where she majored in Elementary Education and furthered her educational career by receiving a master's degree in Administration and Supervision from Nova Southeastern University, and later receiving a Master of Arts degree in Curriculum and Instruction in Reading from Grand Canyon University.

Ms. Moton's unwavering commitment to education has been the impetus for the creation, development and implementation of countless projects throughout Miami Dade County Public Schools. Some of these projects are Science with a Twist (S.W.A.T.) and Bridging Literacy and Science Together, which has benefited many students throughout Miami Dade County Public Schools.

Ms. Moton teaches Honors English and Pre-IB at North Miami Sr. High school. She has been an educator for twenty years and is the developer of the ***Hopes and Fears Book Project*** created to inspire students to write and be bold in the face of adversity during a global pandemic. She is also the author of iRead, iThink, iWrite which was a classroom project developed in 2017 with 9th grade students at Miami Norland Sr. High School.

Tyeshia Bryant

Ms. Tyeshia Bryant was born and raised in sunny Miami, Florida. After graduating from Miami Northwestern Sr. High School, she attended the prestigious University of Florida where she majored in Linguistics and minored in Anthropology. Ms. Bryant taught English as a Second Language through different language schools including Rosetta Stone, where her interest in education sparked. She then went on to become an English Interventionist at Miami Carol City Sr. High where she specialized in test preparation for grades 9-12, including ACT/SAT test prep.

Her devotion to students' success grew profoundly, which motivated Tyeshia into receiving her certification in English and she fully committed herself as an educator. Ms. Bryant teaches at North Miami Senior High School and has previously tutored all high school grade levels for matriculation to Higher Education.

Tyeshia Bryant is more than honored to have taken part in the *Hopes and Fears Book Project*. She is proud to have collaborated in efforts to give her students a platform to share their thoughts and feelings of learning during a global pandemic.

Contributors

Carmello Aurelien
Tchussie Bessard
Derrian Cooper
Thazard Dennis
Sunelisa Desir
Icart Galumette
Roberta Guerrier
Martha Guirola
Cartina Hector
JnLouis Hugens
Serena Jeanmarie
Aimee Jeanty
Valina Jeanty
Ashley Joseph
Lee-Yahna Lawson
Devonne Malcom
Maya Maycock
Juen Michel
Saniyah Mondelus
David Narcisse
Richberth Nelson
Danasia Norville
Sean Paulas
Destinee Pierre
Kayla Richardson
Destiny Rivera
Ludovica Rondelli
Trinity Roselin
Neishalyn Salcedo
Gianina Sanchez
Esther St. Louis
Mysha Uddin
Valencia Williamson

Foreword

I watched closely as students smiled and laughed as they normally would at the conclusion of each school day. I listened as they made plans to see their friends and teachers "tomorrow". They were unaware of the approaching calamity that would change the world as they knew it, and this "tomorrow" they planned for would never come. The world had been "shut down" and they were now trapped inside of their homes.

As a Licensed Clinician, I am mindful of the silent battles fought by students daily. I am aware of the adverse experiences they face that will affect them for the rest of their lives. For these very reasons, worry immediately set in. I worried because not all students come from safe and loving homes. I worried because for many students, school was a safe space. Going to school meant not having to endure physical or emotional abuse for a few hours. It also meant guaranteed meals for the day and being surrounded by friends who made each other feel understood.

With each day that passed, I fretted about the possibility of students' deepest fears becoming heightened. What would happen to all of their hopes, dreams, and aspirations? I found the answer to my question in *Hopes and Fears: Learning academically in a COVID-19 environment.* This book does an exceptional job of capturing the pure and raw emotion felt by students as they learned to adjust and cope with their new sense of normalcy. It portrays our youth's resilience and their ability to persevere in the face of adversity.

Daneisha T. Freeman, LCSW

Acknowledgements

Behind every great school are great leaders who consistently encourage their staff in developing the minds of phenomenal students who aspire to go above and beyond what is expected of them. Therefore, it is with gratitude that we acknowledge Mr. Patrick Lacouty, Principal of North Miami Senior High School, Vice Principal Elvira Ruiz-Carrillo, Assistant Principals Enock Alouidor, Lashawn Gaskins, Terrance Gibson, and Steven Hoskins for their support during this project.

This project has given hope to all students who have a desire to become future authors and have their literary works published.

North Miami Senior High

Carmello Aurelien

Hopes

I hope for a better society
I hope for a better life

Fears

I fear political instability
I fear economic instability

As everything around us crumbles, we grow more worried about
life, about our family, and our well-being.
We are uncertain about what tomorrow will bring us.
We try to cherish every day that passes on
Some of us struggle,
Being blindsided by this virus
We weren't prepared for what has come
Many have lost jobs, homes, and more,
But there is only one thing we can do now and that is have hope;
Hope that everything will get better; hope we can find a
cure soon; hope we stop losing more innocent souls; and hope
we can do this as a community and no longer Fear.

Tchussie Bessard

Hopes

I hope for success in life.

I hope for happier days with positive outcomes and prosperity to come my way.

Fears

I fear neglection from close ones.

I fear disapproval and not being able to be enough.

Hoping is a sweet thing that people do.

It helps stay strong during tuff times that many people endure.

We hope things go our way through many things,

but sometimes seems like too much to ask.

We all have hope; it helps look at things in an optimistic way.

Fear is a very overwhelming thing taking away little bits of faith that you had.

You feel fear going through different things that tears your happiness away from you

Whether its family problems, depression, or even anxiety, fear will always want to take over, but is it only a feeling?

Won't it go away, if you let it?

Derrian Cooper

Hopes

I hope life gets easier
I hope everyone can do some good

Fears

I fear I will not impact this world
I fear people will give up before they have had their chance

I cannot make everyone happy,
That much I know,
But if I can help ease some of the pain people are experiencing
I hope it will do some good
Fear plagues my mind.
Tells me I am not good enough.
It could be true, but I try my hardest,
And that is all that matters anyway.
In the end, a small impact will not satisfy,
I cannot promise it will even do good,
But I tried, and I tried my hardest,
And that is all that matters anyway.

A final message,
To any who reads this
When fears subside
I hope life gets easier.

Thazard Dennis

Hopes

I hope our country comes back twice as strong from the
racial injustice and financial instability.
I hope my family comes out stronger from this year's pandemic.

Fears

I fear that this country will fall into a period of despair from this
quarantine.
I also fear that I will fall into a state of depression.

As we are getting to the closing chapter of this year and COVID-19
has become people's brand-new fear.
Teens faces are on their phones keeping up with the new trends
As we are all suffering in quarantine that seems to never end.
When I look outside my window to be greeted with a facemask that
has people itching, twiddling their thumbs waiting to see what else
COVID-19 has in store.
People are in the streets marching, chanting, and holding up their
signs left and right as the black community continues to stand up and
protest to fight for our civil rights.
A lot of people are claiming that the year 2020 was the worst year of
their life. It's like 2020 is coming and stabbing people in the back
with sharp and pointy knives.

This year has brought a lot of people sorrow, pain, and built-up rage. As the chapter of 2020 is closing, we are opening the year of 2021as a brand-new page.

Sunelisa Desir

Hopes

I hope for today that peace finds its way to every girl and boy.

I fear for today that our voice will not be heard.

Fears

I fear for today that our voice will not be heard.

I fear for today what was lost is now being discovered.

I hope for today that people may have a comprehension on what's
going on in 2020.
I fear for today's society that isn't cooperating with the environment.
I hope for today a better life and future for us and for the
next generations.
I fear for today that we may not have the same privilege as other.
I hope for today that better days are ahead.
I fear for today what was lost is now being discovered.

Icart Galumette

Hopes

I hope that during this time of despair, everyone can find their true meaning of living.

I hope that everyone can get closer to God.

Fears

I fear that being isolated too long will cause stressful households.

I fear that society won't take pandemic seriously and it may cause more deaths.

Let's navigate and go on a tour, despite everything that's happening all around the globe, take a moment to look beyond the actual meaning of Covid-19, the coronavirus. Covid-19 has a deep significance beyond it. It's about being vigorously strong, being there for your family, supporting each other, fighting every step of the way. Covid-19 is about having high hopes, uniting with one another and if applicable, making the last time you have with them memorable. Covid-19 is about having faith that keeps you alive. Ask God to give you the strength to combat and survive during painful, difficult times in life because no one said life would be easy.

Now ask yourself, what is the true meaning of Covid-19? Is it where you find your true self, is it where you thrive, to conquer this fight, and push back, is it where you toughen up and fight back together with your family? Is it where you connect with your family stronger than before or where you fall apart and give up?

Hope is stronger than fear. In tough times is where you discover your true colors and what you capable of accomplishing. Every time Covid-19 strikes, get back up and fight stronger. Only you can defeat yourself by giving in, especially to the coronavirus. Only you can put fear in yourself by not searching for such extraordinary power that you hold. Don't let fear define who you are, don't let the shadows of darkness hide your bravery or confidence.

Why fear when you can overcome adversity and be free? Let the resilience flow naturally. You must go through tough times because that's what forms a new you and defines who you are. That is what makes you confident and unstoppable. The universe works mysteriously; let it work its way through you in efforts to form a new you. The universe can do unexpected things, it might just surprise you! Why embrace Covid-19 when you have the audacity, the power to fight it! Covid-19 is as memorable as the day we were put on this earth, a moment we'll never forget. Keep striving, don't fear, and stand tall in the face of adversity.

Roberta Guerrier

Hopes

Hope is something I lean on to get rid of the fears,

it's an encouragement to look at the world and dream big without

feeling like I'm stepping out of boundaries.

Fears

Fear is a thought process that turns anything positive negative, but at the same time it helps the ones with big ambitions to look overboard and see everything is in your power.

Both HOPE and FEARS are things I'm devoted to like a commander devoting his life to the king and his people. Every day I walk out this palace, my life is always on a thin line with nothing but HOPE and FEARS to hold onto. My family and their peers claim that I'm walking on the right path and I'm doing the right thing. My disciples claim that they envy me because I'm "so" brave and how I overcome any obstacles. But on the other side, they don't know the bright smile, the positive and motivated words, and an optimistic character is nothing but an armor that I wear in HOPE. I always kneel and bow my head whenever I'm facing the king, some think I do it out of respect and some think I do it just to showcase. Little do they know, I do it because of FEAR, I do it because his arms around me is like a scarf that won't come off. To sum it up, HOPE is something that I wear or depend on to hide all the FEARS underneath.

Martha Guirola

Hopes

I hope that despite being positive for the coronavirus, we are all able to overcome hardships - I hope that depression will fade during these times and I'll find peace of mind.

Fears

Catching COVID-19 and putting other lives at risk.
Not being able to be forgiven for causing others to test positive for coronavirus.

People are going through very stressful situations during this pandemic. Fear is upon us all. Many people fear becoming homeless, the death of a relative or close friend, catching coronavirus, not being financially stable, etc. We all at least felt one of these fears so, know you're not alone. Never have any of us thought that we would have to face a pandemic in our lifetime. What scared me the most was how life changed overnight! Many of these fears caused anxiety and depression. We weren't mentally prepared coming into this pandemic with such short notice. We were in school one day, then the next thing you know, we were quarantined within the blink of an eye. Many people panicked and started buying large amounts of certain products like toilet paper, hand sanitizer, and gloves.

Most people thought it was fake at first, nothing to be alarmed about. Then cases started going up, they rushed to the stores and emptied all the shelves, and masks became mandated everywhere! Just know you weren't the only one scared. Many people did not know if they would wake up with electricity or even breakfast. Imagine parents telling their kids that they do not have money for food. For some, having a job is a fear because many people have kids and/or elders at home. They go to work in fear of catching the virus and transmitting it to their family members because the older generation is more likely to die from the virus.

Amid chaos, my biggest fear became a reality. I became a statistic and tested positive for COVID-19. Not only was my life at risk now, but my actions led me to pass on the virus to my mom, and my mom's friend who is an older woman. I feared what would happen to her, I felt so guilty and at fault.

It all started by me going to the park with a friend and his mom had COVID unknown to me. In that moment, I realized just how serious it was to quarantine and abide by the guidelines. I never thought I would get it and that it was super rare to catch. I had a high fever and could not stand up because I was so nauseous. I felt like I was about to faint. Even though the worst thing already happened like catching it and transmitting it to people I care for, I was still worried I would suddenly stop breathing. I was watching the news every day while in quarantine. I think that scared me even more learning about the symptoms and side effects.

After I recovered, my mom still had side effects, and she lost her taste and could not smell anything. I remember her cleaning, and she used a lot of bleach, but she could not smell it. I started crying because the bleach was so strong the dogs began coughing. My mom seemed unfazed since she could not smell anything.

While I had corona, I did not want to stay alone in a room yet, could not be in the same room as my mom. I was scared I did not want to be alone. So, I followed my mom everywhere, even if I felt like fainting. All I could see is big black dots and had blurry vision. My sister then became the head of household because my mom couldn't work. My sister feared not having a job since we depended on her; she had a lot of pressure on her. We are getting through this pandemic together. Although I was down in spirit and we all had our own fears, we used it to unify and strengthen us.

Cartina Hector

Hopes

I hope that this pandemic doesn't hurt any of the dreams that have for future.

I hope that I'm able to focus on school while attending virtually.

Fears

I fear being forgotten because I'm away from family and friends for so long.

I fear my grades dropping and it makes it harder for me to get into college.

Have you ever had the fear of being forgotten by someone you love? It scares me every day. I imagine it being like losing your memory after a terrible accident and those who you love feeling empty because those moments you once treasured are now gone forever.

My sister is all I have; we may not see eye to eye all the time, but that doesn't take away from the love I have for her. While quarantined, I thought about life and how it's going to work out for me. Am I going to be able to finish school and buy my mother the house of her dreams? Am I going to be able to start a career and help pay for my sister's tuition? Or will the pandemic continue, quarantine isolation becomes longer, and I just become a faded memory?

JnLouis Hugens

Hopes

I hope to be successful.

I hope to believe in myself.

Fears

I have the fear of financial instability.

I have the fear of depression.

The word success has different meanings to different people. To me success means, to be happy, to be able to live your life without feeling sorry for yourself. I feel like we all can succeed in life and the key to success is self-belief. Self-belief is one of the most important things that we can possess. I stated that because without self-belief it is easy to give up when we fail in life. Failure maybe a detour, but it is not the end throughout life. We will come across detours, but it is up to us to overcome and keep going. To sum up everything that has been stated thus far, our success is in our hands and it is up to us to face the difficulties that will come throughout our journey to get to where we want to be in life.

Serena Jeanmarie

Hopes

I hope the global pandemic prepared citizens for the unknown

I hope that my family continues to stay healthy

Fears

I fear that the numbers will continue to rise and cause more anxiety

I fear that the virus will hit close to home one day.

March 13, 2020, a date I'll never forget. This is the day my life and many of my peers were transformed. On my way home, I was seated on the passenger seat of my mother's vehicle. She came to get me from school earlier than expected around noon. That's when it truly struck me; my mom never randomly picks me up from school. Education was a key element for her! During school hours, teachers were distributing laptops and many school essentials due to a slight possibility we will not be returning. An alert began to sound off abruptly on everyone's cell phones notifying them that it was officially declared there was, in fact, a global pandemic. That's when I knew my day-to-day life would soon be altered and there would soon be a new normal.

Living through a global pandemic and trying to hold on to every ounce of hope I can grasp onto became draining. Living in a household along with eight anxious beings was not a simple feat. When faced with a deadly disease such as COVID-19, I had to become accustomed to a new form of learning, online school. It was an unfamiliar change that I quickly adapted to. Many people were laid off their work duties which caused many economic panics. One of those workers being my mother, it greatly impacted our source of income. Turning to our religion, Christianity, we prayed nonstop to seek hope and salvation. It was our primary source of protection. We needed and wanted protection from COVID-19 and the great depression that it brought upon society.

To be truly hopeful, filled with hope, during a global pandemic that has killed at least one million people and left many hospitalized, was a trying time. I tried not to dwell on the hardship of my situation and many around me. I chose to view things from an optimistic point of view. I remembered that I had many blessings to be thankful for; my family was COVID free and had shelter. By allowing yourself to view things from an optimistic viewpoint allows you to release serotonin and brings a sense of mindfulness over you.

Aimee Jeanty

Hopes

I hope people will start listening to the guidelines so this can end

I hope I can see my friends again.

Fears

I fear that people will keep being incompetent, combative, denying that somethings are wrong when there clearly isn't.

I fear that I may catch the virus myself

I hope people will start listening to the guidelines so this can end

But I fear that people will keep being incompetent, combative,

denying that somethings wrong when there clearly is

At the beginning

DANGER, WORLDWIDE, VIRAL, CONTAGEOUS

Everyone in the world fearing for their safety

Everyone in the world doing what they can to protect themselves

Except US

We were robbed

Robbed of knowing

Robbed of a year

Robbed of enjoyment

Robbed of very important life

All because he knew and didn't tell us
And all because his followers refuse to listen

We're trying

But having to carry the consequence of others

Going backwards after making progress because so many people don't believe

It makes you want to give up

It is idiotic

Even a child can comprehend

Most of us are trying

But the people that are supposed to be protecting us aren't

Lifting quarantines when cases go down making them surge right back up

Flat out denying that its real

Refusing to set an example and wear a mask

Downplaying the seriousness

How long will this last?

How long will we keep going backwards until some actual change is made

How…long…

Valina Jeanty

Hopes

I hope that we can start getting back to our old lives, without worrying about the effects of COVID-19.

I hope that we will gain peace after all that has been happening in the world.

Fears

I fear that the pandemic will not end fast enough, and I might miss out on many milestones and memories such as prom, birthdays, and holidays.

I fear things will take a while before they go back to normal.

There are times when things happen in your life that will have a major effect on you, but don't fear and worry for things will get better. God always has good things in store for his people. The light will shine and will shine brighter than it ever did before. After this pandemic, there will be peace in our life, and we will get over any problem that the pandemic has brought towards us. One of the things I hope for after this pandemic is that things will get back to normal, and COVID-19 will end very soon. That families will come back together, that little business will open back, that people who are struggling will receive peace once again, and that all dreams are fulfilled and achieved by our heavenly father.

Ashley Joseph

Hopes

I hope we become stable once again.

I hope that we can be able to reunite and socialize the way we used to.

Fears

I fear that the population of mankind will consistently decrease, resulting in an early extinction in the future.

I fear that as soon as this pandemic comes to its end, there will be no normal.

Disease, Disease -
Oh COVID-19, what have you done?
You have prevented us all
From glancing at the bright morning sun.
Threatening our daily lives,
Dispersing our organized agendas,
You are a misery yet to overcome.

Disease, Disease -
Why do you care to disrupt our peace?
Eagerly waiting in line to ride,
Joking out with friends,
Going on a family vacation,
All were a bliss.
As you appear in first sight,

They're all now just a miss.

Disease, Disease -
We may not suffer any longer,
From your preposterous deeds.
You've murdered the innocent lives of many,
But you still do not feel pleased.

Oh, Disease, Disease -
We shall defeat this dare,
Ending it with a pound.
For there is hope.
We shall not stare,
And give it another round.

Lee-Yahna Lawson

Hopes

I hope that this pandemic will change the lives of many
people spiritually and mentally.
I hope that this pandemic will be over and that we will be able to do
the things we love and see the people we care about again in a safe
environment.

Fears

I fear that I might die or someone close to me might die from the
virus.
I fear that the people may not come to realize that god is real
even when they see the situation, they are still blinded to the truth.

Fear is like a chain reaction, but so is hope; it all depends on your perspective on certain situations. You can choose to face it, or you could allow that fear to control your life. Right now, everyone has a common fear whether it is a fear of dying from COVID-19, losing someone to COVID-19 or they are afraid to leave the house. In some way, these fears are connected.

Some people allow themselves to worry and that causes the burden of fear to grow. Do not get me wrong, as individuals, you will worry and have fears at some point, but it should not be what determines who you are.

Fear is like a darkness and hope is like a light, a flame that can blaze with the right fuel. Hope is like a candle that will help you find your way out of the dark. Winds may come but keep lighting that candle back up until you find your way.

It is easier to fear than to hope. It takes courage to overcome those fears and it takes hospitality to share that hope with the world. "For God has not given us the spirit of fear; but of power, and of love, and of a sound mind" (1 Timothy 1:7). Free will is given every man and child, so choose - will it be hope or fear?

Devonne Malcom

Hopes

One day this virus will die off.
I hope that none of my family members would have to experience this virus.

Fears

One of my closest friends might catch the virus.
I fear that one of my family members pass away from the virus.

My fear surrounding this global pandemic would be that I may lose someone very close to me without them knowing how much I love and care about them. This pandemic has done a lot to me and my family, and I refuse to let it continue. My aunt got tested, and found out she used to have the virus, but thank God she didn't experience the symptoms. Overall, I just hope people can take this virus seriously because it can kill, and it is very contagious. The virus has made me become more aware of my surroundings although some people may find this acceptable, I don't because being more aware of my surroundings is good, but we needn't be afraid of going outside. This virus has taken a vile toll on my life, yet the same question still looms in my head, "Will things ever get better?" Of course, one day this will all be over, but what does that say about us? How will we manage? The only being that can answer these questions is the Savior up above; therefore, if we put our trust in Him, who's to say we have nothing else to hope for?

Maya Maycock

Hopes

I hope to become a better individual.
I hope that all my hard work will pay off.

Fears

I fear I will let my fears overcome me.
I fear what society has come to.

Hope is something I pray will help guide my future
The hope of becoming a better individual
The hope that all my sweat and tears will eventually pay off
Not letting my fears control my life.

Hope is something that can bring you out of your darkest moments
Even when there is only a little light
When you fear something, you may not have any control over it
Hope can let you see that little white light in a room full of
darkness.

So, I sit here today, and I pray for more hope.
I pray that I will be a better individual
I pray that our community would not be separated by color
But be united as one.

I pray for the strength and courage to look at my fears and lock them behind a closed door

I pray that all my hardships will pay off.

Juen Michel

Hopes

Some relief and peace of mind
Self-growth for all loved ones during times of isolation

Fears
Corona attacking one of my love ones
Going back to sad times and it grows into depression

Unseeable by the human eye another threat has risen. Not yet truly to be identified, we chose not to keep our distance. Out of the blue, the first victims die. Then another one dies and then day-by-day another mother cries. Watching the news, a sense of fear grumbles inside of me. Ripping and tearing, that same sense of fear then takes over me, bringing this thought to my mind of whether I may be next on the menu. If not me, maybe my family. If not them, maybe others who are also close to me.

Until this day, that sense of fear still roams inside of me, not necessarily by the numbers of those who fell victim, but the nonchalant behavior of society. The thing that hurts me the most is the thought of us being in harm's way mostly because unlike many other threats, this one is not tangible; our forms of defense could only do so much, but not for all of us. Children and elders are still dying, another mother or family still crying. When will this sorrow and weeping of COVID-19 end?

Saniyah Mondelus

Hopes

I hope for aspiration.

I hope for simplicity again.

Fears

I fear what we may become.

I fear the thought of fear.

Hope is such a complex thing and fear is so horrendously dreadful. Fear limits us, it limits us from greatness, opportunity, and adventure. When people hear the word hope they hear "anything is possible if I believe." Based on these last couple of months I can honestly say that all hope is lost. Now all I have is fear, fear that nothing will ever be the same again. Fear that humanity will only keep getting worse. If I did have any hope left in me, I would choose to believe. Choose to believe that this is just a time period in life nothing lasts forever. Then I would ask myself "why does this feel so everlasting?". Everyone has sacrificed so much, how much do we have to sacrifice for things to get better? Many have lost lives, jobs, friends, and most of all hope.

David Narcisse

Hopes

To have a better life
To remain happy when things seem impossible

Fears

Never fear when things appear bleak
Never fear what you can't see

Hope is such a rare, but an abundant thing. Any one person can have it and hope for anything. I personally hope to remain happy and for a better life. This pandemic has caused my hope for these two things to dwindle. I have faith that my hope will sustain and strengthen during and after this pandemic. I have a deep respect for the idea or notion of "hope," because I fear that I will one day lose it.

I am grateful for having hope. Many are unfortunate of being placed in a predicament that has caused them to lose hope. Hope is a great thing and has kept me in good spirits throughout this crazy time. My hopes may sound simplistic, but they have a profound meaning to me. You would have to have been in my shoes to understand why these are my hopes and why I fear losing them.

Richberth Nelson

Hopes

I hope my mom isn't affected in the long run by being positive for the coronavirus

The world implements healthier lifestyles.

Fears

COVID-19 would get worse and we would just have to adjust to it,

Not being able to enjoy my youth because of CDC guidelines and quarantine.

The moment I knew the virus was real was when my mom tested positive. I was shaking uncontrollably, terrified of what might come. I didn't know if I had it, but obviously there was a high chance because I live with her. Four days later, I started getting sick; I had a high fever, and I was coughing. I was about to die, at least, that was the first thing that came to my mind. My whole life flashed in front of my eyes and I had this sunken feeling that everything I want for my future; I might never have. I may never get to accomplish all my dreams!

The thing that kept me going was hope. I knew that during quarantine, I had to get back to my life at some point. After what felt like ten months, I was able to attend school, even though it is virtually. Seeing my friends filled with laughter, cooking and being around my family are the little things that brought me joy. Knowing that I have people who care about me is what keeps me from being depressed during these times.

I miss going out; the wind blowing through my hair, the sounds of the waves crashing at the beach! Hope is knowing that after all of this, I will feel the sand beneath my feet again. I'll have another chance at living a fun, youthful life! These thoughts are motivation to keep me positively thinking about surviving all that comes my way. I hope that COVID ends before December 2021. I want to travel without being scared. I want to feel free! I want to go back to being so full of joy and walking with my head held high. Let your hopes outweigh your fears and know that better days are coming; that's the only way to survive.

Danasia Norville

Hopes

I hope to get closer to God

I hope to be more optimistic

Fears

I fear not improving myself

I fear surviving instead of living

This world is changing,

It is changing drastically.

We can't keep up with this change forever,

We can't fix the damage once it's too late.

Sickness is spreading,

People are dying.

People are working more hours,

Others losing jobs.

Families in bad conditions,

Unable to see loved ones.

People fighting for their lives,

Loved ones helping them fight.

People losing faith,

Others giving up hope.

But sill the world goes round,

Because the fights not over yet.

Sean Paulas

Hopes

I hope for success
I hope for change

Fears
Fear of failure

Fear of success

If you asked me about what I hope for, I would say success
But if you asked me about my fear, success would also be one of
them
Success is not always final
Which is why I fear it more than failure

Failure is something that is common to humans
Failure is the penalty of doing something wrong
If we keep doing what made us successful, we will fail
But what we must know is that failure is not final you can also
gain success

Change can lead to perfection
Change leads to new things
In my opinion there is no downside of change
Change is what the world needs

Destinee Pierre

Hopes

I hope for a better and healthier world
I hope that all my loved ones can stay safe and healthy

Fears

I fear that my family members won't be able to work anymore
I fear that the world will still be toxic

Hope is something I want in the future
I need to have hope during this hard time
I shouldn't give up on the positivity's of life
When tomorrow comes, a brighter day will occur
The beauty of another day living and breathing happily

Fear is something that is on my mind from time to time
Will I still have the benefits of a supportive family?
Will things fall and scatter apart?
Or will there be a better tomorrow?
Do we have to wear masks and stay apart forever?

I do not know how long this pandemic will last
There's no telling if there will be a good or bad outcome
There's no telling of the change that may occur
I will not be a slave to **fear**
I will have **hope**

Kayla Richardson

Hopes

I hope too never be as negative

I hope to be appreciative

Fears

I fear envy

I fear humanity

Everyone is fearful of something

Whether they choose to undermine that fear

Whether they choose to embrace that fear

Fear is a powerful thing

It sometimes holds others back from doing something

Or it causes others to live in trepidation

It even goes as far as having a phobia

Some of the most historical and or iconic people we know today

once or still have feared something

From Matin Luther King Jr. to Beyonce, who might seem so far

apart but are connected in more ways than one.

They all are afraid.

I fear humanity and what we have become, we will never be the

Utopia that some work so hard to create

People choose to have hate, anger, envious. When that will get you

nowhere in the long run

Holding on to negative energy, can only lead to negative or envious

behaviors. And who is that really helping?

Choose to be appreciative of what you have and not envy what the next person has.

Destiny Rivera

Fear- I am struggling; not only me, but my family and many more students who can relate to me. Personally, I am struggling with depression. Life is so hard at this point I don't know if I could believe in myself again, I don't know if I will have another chance for anything I want anymore.

Hope- I hope I could believe in myself and chase my dreams more than ever, I just want to believe and know that there is still a chance for me to get to where I want in the future, If there's a future that is. I JUST WISH EVERYTHING WOULD GO BACK TO NORMAL!!!

Hopes and fears-

At this point I fear for my life, for the people and everything around me. I fear! There's no telling if you live another day or not. I risk my life for an education so I can be somebody one day, but seeing what the world must bring, I fear it's not worth it. Ever since this ... I don't feel the same anymore. I am not motivated, and I have lost hope in everything; it's bringing me to a depressing moment in my life where I can't motivate myself. I know I'm not the only one who feels this type of way, we are going through the same thing.

I wake up in the morning every day to risk my life for and education I don't know is going to be worth it anymore. I can't do online, that's not a choice for me. If I do online, I would not even have a chance to pass, so I have no choice but to risk my life and come to school not knowing if someone in my class is sick or not. Not knowing if I will live to see another day. You can't cough or sneeze like you used to; if you do, suddenly you are infected. I understand that people are trying to do good and be safe, but that's not fair to the people who don't really have it and just have allergies.

This is not earth! Sometimes I feel like I'm on another planet where people having chances and choices are not an option anymore. I don't like it here, I want to have hope again and know that there's a chance for me to live to see another day and to get my education without my life having to be at risk for me to do something good for myself. I just want to have faith in myself again, I just want to know that everything is going to be perfectly fine and that I have an option to do good.

Ludovica Rondelli

Hopes

The numbers of cases will decrease
We would be able to go outside and travel without any
complications/obstacles.

Fears

We will not be able to return to our usual routines and enjoy life
without a mask anytime soon
A cure will not be discovered, and we wouldn't be able to travel
before Summer 2021.

2020 was a difficult and unexpected year,
That brought innumerable moments of tears.
However, no matter all the despair and rage,
Hope will never fade.
We hope for better events
That will show the world benevolence.
Events that will motivate and inspire,
All the generations to finally, execute what's required.
If we work together, and don't lose hope,
We will be able to go back to our free life all around the globe.
Families will ultimately be able to reunite,
And finally hug each other so tight.
The barriers within us and the rest of the world will lastly,
dismantle.

Thanks to the hope and the unified fight against this vicious battle.

Yes, this year was a challenge and a test

That we passed with readiness.

Trinity Roselin

Hopes

I hope we find a cure for COVID-19
I hope people stop getting very sick

Fears

Covid-19 will have an impact, even in the future.
People who have taken the Covid-19 vaccine begin to die from it.

Covid-19 has caused many deaths, stress, and anxiety on many people and the world to go into a global economic shut down. Now, I know that most people would mainly have fears about Covid-19, but as for me, I have hope. As of now, you may be confused or wondering why I have hope about Covid-19. Even though Covid-19 has put us through a lot, it has brought some good. For example, it has brought families closer, helped people find who they are, or even learn new things.

Neishalyn Salcedo

Hopes

I hope that I can keep the calmness that I found during the pandemic

I hope that everyone heals mentally

Fears

I fear others falling ill from stress and anxiety

I fear we can't go back to normal

The coronavirus is something we cannot see nor touch but it hurts us tremendously. Mental health and loneliness are something that has hurt me. Along with the hope of calmness, I wish to find the person I truly am in the midst of everything. I never thought I'll be so affected and learn so much from something that has a negative stigma. Mental health is something that's very important to me so to see it take such a drastic turn is something that scared me. I didn't know I'd feel so lost during this time of fear. Never thought I'd have the feeling of emptiness in such a short period of time. I didn't laugh with anyone, didn't talk, and didn't open up to anyone. In a way, the calmness that I searched for was found. The feeling of knowing you don't have to be nervous about certain things because you're at home with yourself and finding comfort in that is what kept me sane. I am now finding me, the person who was so scared to be someone that they lost themselves during this whole craziness. Although we are in the middle of something so dark, I still found some light.

Gianina Sanchez

My hope during this pandemic...

Is to stay healthy and that everything will go back to normal

My fear during this pandemic...

Is that I will lose someone important to me and get sick

During this whole pandemic, I have kept my hope and faith that everything will go back to normal sooner or later. Though at times we may fear that things will stay like this forever, we must have hope that things will go back to normal. The first few months in quarantine were okay, but the more I stayed stuck at home, the more my anxiety took over me. The first time I left my house since being stuck inside for almost 3 months, I was shaking because I had not been around people in a while. When online school started, I had a panic attack before a Zoom meeting, and I could not believe what happened. Thankfully, I breathed in and out and managed to calm myself down. This whole pandemic has been a drastic change we were not prepared for, but if we want things to end, we must stay strong and have hope.

Guilt, a shame we cannot escape.

Doesn't discriminate, taking the lives of many.

Clinging on to you like a scared child.

Sticking with you like white on rice.

Having thoughts u cannot escape.

Masking it up so no one knows man it's a shame.

A tough battle you feel you cannot erase.

Speak up, know it's not your fault you CAN change.

Get help.

Denial. Anger. Bargaining. Depression.

Overcome this unbearable cycle of reckless pain.

Esther St. Louis

Hopes

That everyone makes it out happier than when this started

To reunite with family and friends

Fears

I fear that we will have a new normal that's uncomfortable

Someone close to me not being able to survive

Destressing During a Pandemic (Ways to Have Fun)

Staying at home during a pandemic can be bored, stressful, and annoying. So, to solve the issue, here are 4 ways to destress during a pandemic at home.

At-home Laser Maze

It may sound weird and unachievable but all you need are household supplies. You will need two rolls of duct tape of any color, and a hallway. Connect the tape from wall to wall and build as you go; you can make it how big or small. Turn the lights off, use flashlights or LED lights and find your way through the maze!

Build a Fort

You can use whatever pillows and blankets you'd like. All you really need is an empty space, some chairs, sheets and if you want to make it cute you can add LED lights! To make it even more enjoyable, bring in your laptop and snacks to "Netflix & Relax".

Draw or Paint

Drawing and painting are one of the top ways to destress and clear your mind! You can express your feelings and thought as you are drawing, and you don't need much to do so! All you need are a few sheets of paper, markers or coloring pencils. For painting, you can use markers, water, a paint brush, and sheets of paper or any canvas that would be acceptable such as old shoes and notebooks. This can be done by sitting the marker in water and let it soak for few minutes until the water turns the color of the marker. Then, dip the brush in the water and let your imagination run wildly on your canvas.

Family Night

You guys can pick out a movie to watch or board games to play. This will allow you to forget about everything that's going on around you to make some fun and memorable moments with you family.

Mysha Uddin

Hopes

To safely reunite with my family

To be able to go out without being scared

Fears
Contracting the virus

Losing a family member or friend

"The Evacuation"

My family and I had been living in Bangladesh (a small country with a high population exceeding 162 million people) for more than 7 years. When COVID-19 hit, it got extremely scary. In Bangladesh, good doctors and good hospitals aren't as easily accessible. We were fearful that the worst may happen. My father did what he had to do to protect his family: we had an emergency evacuation from Bangladesh to the United States by the US embassy; it was the most nerve-wracking experience of my life.

The coronavirus not only frightened the people of my country but my immediate household as well because of its attack on the upper-respiratory system. Both my mom and my brother grew up living with Asthma. This sent my family into a frenzy. We contacted the US embassy because we knew coming to The United States meant that there would be better doctors in case anyone in my family were to get the virus. An emergency plane was then chartered for all American Citizens which gave us our first sense of hope.

We had 12 hours between March 30th-March 31st to gather all our possessions and make it back to the airport. We took the only choice we had which was to leave everything behind: all our furniture, our house, our clothes and move back to North America. Later that night, we were informed that our plane wasn't taking off from Shahjalal International Airport until 6:00 pm and that if we were going to be hungry, we had to bring our own food and any toiletries we would need, including toilet paper because everything would be closed. We terrified at the airport, not knowing who had the virus or not!

The US Ambassador came to see off the US citizens as we went through 3 check points. They asked screening questions about recent illnesses and who we were around, it felt like a scene from a movie. Our family members and friends sent us off with food and it dawned on me that no one knew when would be the next time that we'll see them.

We sanitized everything and made sure we social distanced as we arrived on the plane, ready to embark on our journey that was at least a 24-hour plane ride. After landing in the United States, it was freezing cold at Dulles International Airport in Virginia; it was also a ghost town! The entire experience was very weird, frightening, on top of that we were jetlagged.

Everything that my family experienced on that voyage caused true paranoia. For that, we made sure that we self-quarantined for a month then made our way to Miami, Florida. COVID-19 has affected everyone globally; it is not a joke! Hopefully, soon enough, we will be safely reunited with our loved ones and this, too, shall pass.

Valencia Williamson

Hopes

I hope to be able to go out again

I hope for change in our society

Fears

I fear for our people

I fear that this pandemic will not end for now

My hopes and fears

Hope is something that you dream

Not only dream about but believe in

I hope for lots of things

But then my hope fades away

Because I realize what our world has become

Our world has gone to violence and discrimination

This pandemic is turning us mad

People are getting more and more bitter towards each other

We are not the same as we use to be

This pandemic has changed us, and we stop hoping

I don't know what to expect anymore

I just hope for change and for us to be United as one

So much pain and suffering is happening that is unforgettable

But we should not stop hoping for a better and brighter day

And you shall find hope because I am starting to find hope.

Figure 1A typical day in the classroom

Figure 2 Engaged in interactive learning with Technology

Figure 3 Critical Thinking

Figure 4 A New Normal

Challenges and Successes: In the Classroom

Challenges:

Attendance is number one, we talk with students, but then you don't see them for another week or two.

Consistency with students' level of engagement, sometimes we're unable to make eye contact.
Level of understanding, we can't gauge the level of facial expressions due to MSO.

Completion of work may not be done due to their understanding or they're out of their comfort zone because they are relaxing at home. Students show up to class but won't do the work. It's very frustrating during the grading process. Making connections/building student-teacher rapport, building personal students' connections (are barriers due to unfamiliarity).
Students don't really engage due to their comfort level; some students are physically with you, so they aren't as comfortable to speak up.

Successes:

Increase the level of activities to promote critical thinking skills
Virtual schools offer more technical activities; therefore, creating tech savvy students.
Allows more logical activities rather than the average stand/sit
Students are more vocal, forces you to share in class, willing to share because they are behind the screen.

ESOL students pick up on language; they are effective due to non-verbal cues are not there to rely on, so it forces them to use the language more and speak up.

Students become their own advocate and share with teachers what works in other classrooms to see if they can implement their way of working in other virtual classes.

Sharing best practices among students and conducting peer-to-peer reviews.

Resources are centralized in one location whether it is from home or school; it saves money (cost efficient paper, toner, ink, etc.), more organized, able to load and prepare assignment quicker for student accessibility. (Streamline resources) Paperless, new way of teaching, fluidity (can teach from anywhere, if need be) via Zoom or other virtual communication platforms. Always sharing best practices with teachers.

5 ways to increase Hope during a global pandemic

1. **Stay organized**: use a planner or a calendar to keep track of assignment due dates so they are not rushing to complete many or large assignments at the last minute.

2. **Practice Self-Care**: self-care is anything you enjoy that makes you feel good. Anything that puts you in a positive mood (Music, exercising, video games, deep breathing, talking to friends, arts & crafts, watching a movie or favorite tv shows, etc.)

3. **Don't be afraid to ask for help**: it's okay to not understand. Don't feel that you must know everything. For things that you're unsure of seek assistance from someone who you think could help (classmates, family, teachers).

4. **Learn your physical signs of stress**: what happens to you when you're feeling stressed? Your body will send you signals (headache, fatigue, decreased or increased appetite, sleeplessness, irritability, etc.). Be aware of these signals so that you can start stress relief activities to combat them.

5. **Hygiene**: If you're attending school physically and are concerned with contracting COVID, stay 6 ft away from others, wear your masks, wash your hands often, use hand sanitizer. Find comfort in knowing you are doing your part in helping to keep yourself and others safe.

Stress

- Remain calm
- Talk to people you trust
- Maintain a healthy lifestyle
- Engage in physical activity
- Avoid drinking alcohol, smoking, tobacco, or the use of other substances
- Maintain regular sleeping habits
- Feeling overwhelmed – talk to a counselor or health care work
- Avoid listening to unreliable resources and/or disinformation
- Limit exposure to news coverage
- Apply previously learned strategies

Fatigue

- Eliminate negative coping skills
- Maintain a routine
- Keep a daily gratitude journal
- Listen to motivational videos
- Practice mindfulness
- Implement a self-care regimen
- Breathe and grieve; have a support system in place

Isolation

- Reach Out: Ask, Listen, Encourage
- Check in with loved ones

- Schedule a virtual hangout
- Go for a walk
- Lend a helping hand
- Use social media wisely
- Tap into available resources

Coping skills to destress while being quarantined

Deep Breathing Exercises
Inhale slowly for 4 seconds as if you're smelling a flower. Pause.

Exhale slowly for 4 seconds as if you're blowing a leaf.

Grounding Exercises
Using your five senses, look around and identify 5 things you can

see, 4 things you can feel, 3 things you can smell, 2 things you can

hear, and 1 thing you can taste.

Take a timeout
Retreat to a place away from the thing that is causing you distress.

This should be a place that makes you feel calm and at peace.

Know your triggers
What are the things that cause you to feel angry, sad, anxious,
worried, etc.?

Pay attention to physiological changes *(Physical changes in your body)*
Sweating, shaking, increased heart rate, turning red, crying, etc.

Positive peer support
Engage with friends who you trust, feel safe with, encourage you to
do well, and whom you are comfortable talking to.

Positive self-talk
I can do this. I will get through this. I am smart. I am brave. I am

enough. I have a purpose. I am valuable. Etc.

Journaling
Use a journal to write down all the things you would like to tell

someone but are unable to. Think of this journal as your friend

who's going to protect all your secrets and give you a safe space to

vent.

Music
Listen to your favorite tunes.

Exercise
Go for a walk, run, jump rope, swim, yoga, etc.

Practice a hobby
Gaming, puzzles, dancing, sports, arts & crafts, etc.

Progressive muscle relaxation
Start at your feet, curl your toes into the bottom of your feet to create tension (not to the point of pain), hold for 5 seconds and then release. Repeat these steps for each part of your body until you reach the top. Focus on the discomfort from the tension and then the relaxation you feel when you release.

Practice self-care
Shower daily, brush your teeth, wear clean clothes, fix your hair, eat healthy meals, get a good night's sleep

Practice Gratitude
What are three things you are thankful for? What is something good that happened to you today? Who is someone you appreciate?

Mindfulness
Meditation: While engaging in deep breathing exercises, focus on a particular object or activity such as your breath entering and leaving your body or the sound of a clock ticking. Focus on this only. If your mind begins to wander, refocus your attention.

Focus on your strengths
Brave, loving, honest, persistent, funny, optimistic, forgiving, patient, leader, creative, athletic, etc.

Be organized
Create a daily schedule or routine, use a planner, set alarms, etc.

Set Boundaries
It's okay to say "no".

Healthy thinking
Mistakes happen and are an inevitable part of life. Try not to dwell on mistakes you have made. Acknowledge the mistake and then determine what you could do differently the next time.

Engaging Activities

1. Write an essay about the current Hopes and Fears that you are facing.

2. Create a T-chart of the current emotions that you feel about your Hopes and Fears and ways to work on them.

3. Make a mindfulness Tik-Tok demonstrating ways to destress and meditate at the end of a school-day.

4. Create a Flipgrid campaign informing others of ways to stay safe and practice CDC guidelines.

5. Create a visual Padlet timeline to visually express the different moods you experienced while being quarantined.

6. Incorporate Growth Mindset strategies/bellringers.

7. Draw a collage/poster tribute to the Essential Frontline Workers.

8. Create a song, rap, poem, short story, or a news report that summarizes your personal experiences during a global pandemic.

9. Conduct an interview with your peers about coping strategies that they have been implementing in their daily lives.

10. Create a newsletter that can be distributed monthly address the latest developments surrounding schools, front-line workers, testing sites and more.

Journaling/Notes:

References

www.paho.org

www.who.int

www.paho.org/coronavirus

https://www.today.com/health/7-self-care-tips-coping-covid-19-
crisis-fatigue-t189933

https://www.mass.gov/info-details/managing-isolation-and-
loneliness-during-covid-19

Resources

National Suicide Prevention Hotline: 1-800-273-TALK (8255)

Crisis Text Line: Text "HELLO" to 741741

SAMHSA (Substance Abuse and Mental Health Services Administration)'s National Helpline: 1-800-662-HELP (4357)

Made in the USA
Las Vegas, NV
18 June 2021